# The Enlightened Path to Project Success

## Leadership Lessons from the Bhagavad Gita

Suswaram **Sridhar**

Feb 2024

# Table of Contents

This structure offers a comprehensive guide for project managers to navigate the complexities of modern leadership with the age-old wisdom of the Bhagavad Gita, providing both practical strategies and spiritual insights for personal and professional development.

# Preface

In the ever-evolving landscape of project management, where complexity meets the constant drive for innovation and efficiency, the quest for a guiding light is perennial. It is in this pursuit that we turn to an ancient source of wisdom, the Bhagavad Gita, a timeless scripture that has guided countless souls on the path of duty, righteousness, and self-realization. "The Enlightened Path to Project Success: Leadership Lessons from the Bhagavad Gita" is an endeavour to bridge the profound teachings of the Gita with the pragmatic world of project management.

This book is born out of a realization that the challenges faced by modern project managers are not just logistical or technical but deeply philosophical and ethical. The Bhagavad Gita, with its universal teachings on duty, action without attachment, the balance of the three gunas, and the pursuit of wisdom, offers invaluable insights into leadership, teamwork, decision-making, and personal growth.

The journey of writing this book has been one of exploration and discovery, seeking to translate the Gita's ancient verses into actionable strategies for today's project leaders. Each chapter delves into a specific teaching of the Gita, exploring its relevance to the challenges and opportunities faced by project managers. From embracing duty and ethical decision-making to cultivating resilience, adaptability, and compassion, the book aims to illuminate the path to enlightened leadership and project success.

Our goal is to inspire project managers to look beyond the immediate demands of timelines and targets, to lead with a sense of higher purpose, wisdom, and equanimity. It is an invitation to integrate spiritual principles into the fabric of professional life, transforming the act of managing projects into an opportunity for personal and collective growth.

"The Enlightened Path to Project Success" is not just a guide to managing projects more effectively; it is a manifesto for transforming leadership through the timeless wisdom of the Bhagavad Gita. Whether you are a seasoned project manager or just embarking on your leadership journey, this book offers a new perspective on navigating the complexities of projects and people with grace, integrity, and a deep sense of purpose.

As you turn the pages, we hope you find inspiration, insight, and the courage to lead your projects—and indeed, your life—with the enlightened wisdom of the Bhagavad Gita. Welcome to a journey of transformation, where the ancient and the modern converge to create a new paradigm of leadership and success.

Let us embark on this journey together, with open hearts and minds, ready to discover the profound impact of the Gita's teachings on our professional practices and personal lives.

# Dedication

*This book is crafted for **every Project Manager** who aspires to transform their life and achieve remarkable growth and contributions in their career.*

# About Suswaram **Sridhar**

Suswaram Sridhar embodies the rare fusion of deep technological expertise and profound philosophical insight, making him a luminary in both the realms of information technology and leadership development. With an illustrious career spanning over 33 years, including pivotal roles as a Chief Information Officer (CIO) for more than a decade, Sridhar has not only led transformative IT initiatives but has also pioneered the integration of timeless wisdom into modern management practices.

Residing in the vibrant city of Hyderabad, India, Sridhar's professional journey is a testament to his visionary leadership and innovative thinking. His tenure as a CIO is marked by remarkable achievements in deploying advanced IT solutions, spearheading digital transformation projects, and cultivating IT environments that align with and amplify organizational objectives.

However, what truly sets Sridhar apart is his passionate dedication to mentoring the next generation of project management professionals. Drawing upon the rich teachings of the Bhagavad Gita, he has adeptly translated ancient philosophical concepts into actionable strategies for today's dynamic project management landscape. His workshops and mentorship programs are renowned for their ability to inspire professionals to navigate both personal and professional challenges with wisdom, integrity, and resilience.

Sridhar's profound understanding of the Bhagavad Gita has not only enriched his own life but has also illuminated the paths of countless others. He skilfully applies the scripture's teachings on duty, detachment, and discernment to cultivate leadership qualities that transcend conventional success metrics, advocating for a leadership style that is grounded in ethical principles, mindfulness, and a commitment to the greater good.

An acclaimed speaker and thought leader, Sridhar's contributions extend beyond organizational boundaries to influence the broader discourse on the integration of spiritual principles in business and leadership. His insights into the application of the Bhagavad Gita's wisdom in addressing modern-day dilemmas have garnered him widespread respect and admiration.

Through his mentorship, Sridhar continues to inspire a new wave of leaders capable of leading with compassion, vision, and a deep sense of purpose. His legacy is defined not just by technological advancements and project successes, but by the indelible impact of his teachings on the personal and professional growth of individuals across the globe.

# Introduction

In an era where the pace of change is relentless and the scope of projects ever-expanding, the quest for enduring wisdom to navigate the professional and personal spheres becomes paramount. This search leads us to the ancient yet timeless teachings of the Bhagavad Gita, a treasure trove of spiritual and practical wisdom that remains as relevant today as it was thousands of years ago. The Gita offers profound insights into duty, leadership, decision-making, and the art of living, making it an invaluable guide for modern project managers and leaders striving for excellence.

This book bridges the millennia-old wisdom of the Bhagavad Gita with contemporary project management challenges, presenting a unique blend of spiritual philosophy and practical strategies. It aims to inspire project managers to transcend traditional leadership paradigms, fostering an approach that is rooted in ethical principles, mindfulness, and a deep sense of purpose. Through the lens of the Gita, readers are invited to explore the virtues of duty, detachment, wisdom, and compassion, applying these timeless principles to achieve both project success and personal growth.

As we embark on this journey, we delve into how the teachings of the Bhagavad Gita can illuminate the path of leadership in today's complex and dynamic environment, offering clarity amidst chaos and instilling a sense of calm determination. Welcome to a transformative exploration of leadership, where ancient wisdom meets modern practice, guiding us towards enlightened management and a fulfilling life.

# Chapter 1: Duty and Dharma in Project Management

## Introduction:

In the realm of project management, understanding and fulfilling one's duty (dharma) is crucial. This chapter explores how the ancient concept of dharma from the Bhagavad Gita can be applied to modern project management, offering a foundation for ethical leadership and effective decision-making.

## The Essence of Dharma:

Dharma, in the context of the Bhagavad Gita, refers to the righteous path or duty that everyone is obligated to follow. It is the moral law that guides one's actions for the welfare of society and personal spiritual growth. In project management, dharma can be seen as the ethical obligations and responsibilities that a project manager must uphold to ensure the success and integrity of a project.

## Applying Dharma in Project Management:

1. Understanding Your Role:

   - Each project manager must introspect to understand their role not just as a leader, but as a facilitator, mentor, and visionary for their team and project.

2. Ethical Decision-Making:

   - Decisions should be made not only based on outcomes but also on the ethical implications, considering the welfare of the team, stakeholders, and the larger community.

3. Commitment to Project Goals:

   - Aligning personal actions with the project's goals, ensuring dedication to the project's success while maintaining integrity and transparency.

## Illustration: The Dharma Wheel

Imagine the project as a chariot, the team members as horses, and the project manager as the charioteer. The dharma wheel represents the ethical framework and values guiding the chariot's path. Just as a charioteer directs the horses with a steady hand, a project manager guides the project to success through adherence to dharma.

## Table: Dharma in Action

| Aspect of Project Management | Application of Dharma |
|---|---|
| Leadership | Leading with integrity, honesty, and transparency. |

| Aspect of Project Management | Application of Dharma |
|---|---|
| Decision-Making | Making decisions that are ethical and beneficial for all stakeholders. |
| Conflict Resolution | Resolving conflicts with fairness and compassion. |
| Risk Management | Assessing and managing risks with foresight and responsibility. |
| Resource Allocation | Distributing resources equitably and efficiently. |

## The Impact of Dharma on Team Dynamics:

Adhering to one's dharma creates a positive and ethical work environment, fostering trust and respect among team members. It encourages open communication, collaboration, and a collective sense of purpose. When the project manager embodies these principles, it inspires the team to follow suit, leading to improved morale and project outcomes.

## Conclusion

Incorporating the concept of dharma into project management not only elevates the role of the project manager but also transforms the project team and the work they do into a cohesive, ethical, and successful endeavor. This chapter has laid the groundwork for understanding how ancient wisdom can inform and enhance modern project management practices, setting the stage for deeper exploration in subsequent chapters.

# Chapter 2: The Art of Selfless Action in Leadership

## Introduction:

This chapter delves into the Bhagavad Gita's teachings on Karma Yoga, the path of selfless action, and its implications for project management. It highlights how project managers can lead with a focus on action, devoid of attachment to outcomes, fostering a team environment that is both productive and harmonious.

## Key Concepts:

1. **Selfless Action:** Acting without attachment to the fruits of the action.

2. **Dedication to Duty:** Performing one's duty for the duty's sake, not for personal gain.

3. **Equanimity:** Maintaining mental balance in success and failure.

## The Importance of Selfless Action in Project Management:

- **Promotes Team Unity:** When the leader focuses on the action rather than the reward, it sets a precedent for the team, encouraging collaboration over competition.

- **Enhances Job Satisfaction:** Team members find greater satisfaction in their work when they perceive their efforts as contributing to a larger purpose.

- **Improves Project Outcomes:** Detachment from the results helps in making more rational, less emotionally biased decisions.

## Action Items for Project Managers:

- Lead by example, demonstrating selflessness in action.

- Encourage team members to focus on their roles and responsibilities, rather than obsessing over rewards or recognition.

- Cultivate an environment where success is celebrated as a collective achievement and setbacks are viewed as learning opportunities.

**Table: Implementing Selfless Action**

| Aspect | Traditional Approach | Selfless Action Approach |
| --- | --- | --- |
| **Goal Setting** | Focused on achieving personal or team recognition | Set goals that align with the larger mission of the organization |
| **Decision Making** | Driven by personal biases and desires | Make decisions based on what is best for the project and team |

| Aspect | Traditional Approach | Selfless Action Approach |
|---|---|---|
| Feedback | Often seen as personal criticism | Viewed as an opportunity for growth and improvement |
| Success | Celebrated as an individual achievement | Recognized as a collective effort and shared with the team |
| Failure | Viewed as a personal setback | Seen as a learning experience and a step towards future success |

## Illustration: The Cycle of Selfless Action

This section would include a conceptual diagram illustrating the cycle of selfless action in project management, showing how actions rooted in duty and detached from personal gain led to improved team dynamics, project outcomes, and personal growth.

## Diagram for Chapter Two: The Art of Selfless Action in Leadership

*Please imagine a circular diagram with the following elements:*

1. **Centre:** The Project Manager, symbolizing the source of leadership and action.

2. **First Outer Layer:** Key actions - Planning, Executing, Monitoring.

3. **Second Outer Layer:** Selfless action principles - Focus on duty, Equanimity in success and failure, Collective achievement.

4. **Outermost Layer:** Outcomes - Enhanced team unity, Improved project outcomes, Personal growth and satisfaction.

# Chapter 3: Achieving Equanimity Amidst Project Turbulence

## Introduction:

In the fast-paced and often unpredictable world of project management, equanimity — the ability to maintain mental calmness, composure, and evenness of temper, especially in difficult situations — becomes a cornerstone for effective leadership. This chapter explores how teachings from the Bhagavad Gita on maintaining equanimity can be applied to navigate the ups and downs of project management.

## The Concept of Equanimity in the Bhagavad Gita:

Equanimity, or "Sthira Sukham," as referred to in the Bhagavad Gita, emphasizes the importance of remaining steadfast and balanced, irrespective of the outcomes of one's actions. For a project manager, this means leading with a focus on action and effort rather than being overly attached to the results.

# Key Areas for Application:

1. **Decision Making:** Making balanced decisions based on rational thinking rather than emotional reactions.

2. **Team Management:** Leading teams with a steady hand, providing support during successes and failures alike.

3. **Stakeholder Engagement:** Managing expectations and communicating with stakeholders in a balanced and transparent manner.

**Table: Strategies for Maintaining Equanimity**

| Strategy | Application in Project Management |
|---|---|
| **Mindful Leadership** | - Practice mindfulness to stay present and focused.<br>- Lead with awareness and intention, keeping the bigger picture in mind. |
| **Balanced Response to Outcomes** | - Celebrate successes without overindulgence.<br>- Learn from failures without despair. |
| **Steadfast Focus on Goals** | - Keep the project objectives in clear view, guiding team efforts towards these goals.<br> - Avoid being swayed by short-term fluctuations or challenges. |
| **Effective Stress Management** | - Employ stress-reduction techniques for yourself and your team.<br> - Foster a supportive and positive work environment. |
| **Adaptive and Flexible Planning** | - Be prepared to adjust plans based on evolving project needs.<br>- Encourage innovation and creative problem-solving within the team. |

## Achieving Equanimity Through Communication:

Effective communication is vital in maintaining equanimity within project teams. Transparent, honest, and timely communication helps in managing expectations, mitigating conflicts, and fostering a culture of trust and respect.

## Practicing Equanimity in Stakeholder Engagement:

Engaging stakeholders with a balanced approach ensure that their expectations are managed realistically. It involves being honest about project potentials and limitations, thereby building trust and credibility.

## Equanimity and Personal Growth:

Equanimity is not just a professional asset but also a personal virtue that contributes to overall well-being. It aids in personal development, enhancing one's ability to handle life's challenges with grace and resilience.

## Conclusion:

Equanimity in project management is about leading with a calm, composed mindset, focused on diligent effort rather than fluctuating outcomes. It's about steering the project ship through turbulent waters with a steady hand and a clear vision, ensuring that both the team and the project can navigate challenges successfully.

The teachings of the Bhagavad Gita on equanimity offer timeless wisdom that, when applied to the realm of project management, can transform the way projects are led and executed. This chapter aims to provide project managers with practical strategies to cultivate equanimity, thereby enhancing their leadership effectiveness and the overall success of their projects.

# Chapter 4: Cultivating Sattva for Team Excellence

## Introduction:

In the dynamic environment of project management, the concept of Sattva, representing qualities of harmony, balance, and purity, becomes essential for fostering team excellence. This chapter delves into how the Sattvic qualities described in the Bhagavad Gita can be cultivated within project teams to enhance productivity, creativity, and well-being.

## Understanding Sattva:

Sattva is one of the three gunas (qualities) in Hindu philosophy, characterized by wisdom, harmony, and goodness. In the context of project management, cultivating a Sattvic environment means creating a workspace that promotes clarity, ethical practices, and a positive, collaborative team culture.

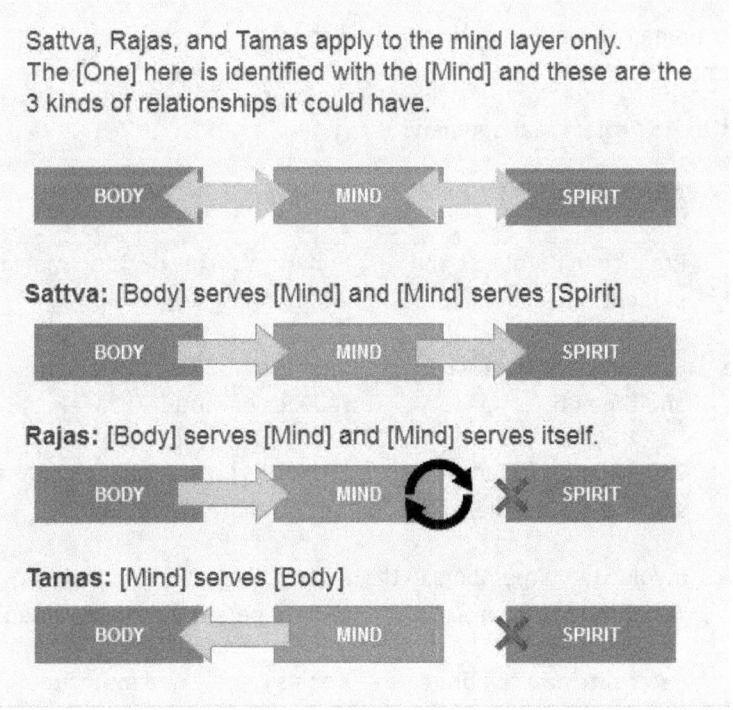

Sattva, Rajas, and Tamas apply to the mind layer only. The [One] here is identified with the [Mind] and these are the 3 kinds of relationships it could have.

BODY ⬌ MIND ⬌ SPIRIT

**Sattva:** [Body] serves [Mind] and [Mind] serves [Spirit]

BODY ➡ MIND ➡ SPIRIT

**Rajas:** [Body] serves [Mind] and [Mind] serves itself.

BODY ➡ MIND ↻ ✕ SPIRIT

**Tamas:** [Mind] serves [Body]

BODY ⬅ MIND ✕ SPIRIT

# Key Strategies for Cultivating Sattva:

1. **Promoting a Positive Work Environment:**

   - Encourage open communication and mutual respect among team members.
   - Create a physically and psychologically safe workspace.

2. **Encouraging Ethical Practices:**

   - Lead by example, demonstrating integrity and fairness in all actions.
   - Implement transparent processes for decision-making and conflict resolution.

3. **Fostering Team Learning and Growth:**

   - Provide opportunities for professional development and continuous learning.
   - Encourage knowledge sharing and collaboration across the team.

**Table: Sattvic Practices in Project Management**

| Sattvic Practice | Application | Benefits |
| --- | --- | --- |
| Mindful Leadership | Practice mindfulness and presence in leadership. | Enhances focus, decision-making, and reduces stress. |
| Healthy Work-Life Balance | Encourage flexible schedules and time off. | Increases job satisfaction and reduces burnout. |
| Constructive Feedback | Offer feedback that is specific, actionable, and kind. | Promotes growth and improvement without harming morale. |
| Inclusive Decision-Making | Involve team members in the decision-making process. | Builds team unity and ensures diverse perspectives are valued. |
| Celebration of Successes | Recognize and celebrate team achievements. | Boosts morale and motivates continued excellence. |

## Cultivating Sattva Through Daily Practices:

- **Morning Check-ins:** Start the day with a brief team meeting to set intentions and focus.

- **Gratitude Practices:** Encourage team members to share something they're grateful for, enhancing positivity.

- **Learning Sessions:** Regularly schedule sessions where team members can learn from each other or external experts.

## Overcoming Challenges with Sattva:

Implementing Sattvic practices in the midst of project deadlines and pressures requires mindfulness and dedication. It involves balancing the drive for results with the well-being of the team, ensuring that productivity does not come at the cost of team morale or ethical standards.

## Conclusion:

Cultivating Sattva within project teams is not merely about achieving immediate project goals but about fostering an environment where creativity, ethical behaviour, and well-being are prioritized. This holistic approach not only leads to successful project outcomes but also contributes to the personal growth and satisfaction of team members, creating a virtuous cycle of excellence and harmony.

By integrating the principles of Sattva into project management practices, leaders can transform their teams into high-performing units that operate with wisdom, harmony, and balance. This chapter provides a roadmap for nurturing these qualities, ensuring that project teams can thrive in today's complex and fast-paced business environment.

# Chapter 5: The Power of Detachment and Dispassion

## Introduction:

Chapter Five delves into the transformative power of detachment and dispassion in project management. Drawing from the Bhagavad Gita's teachings, this chapter explores how embodying detachment from outcomes and dispassion towards temporary successes and failures can lead to more effective, resilient, and mindful project leadership.

## Understanding Detachment and Dispassion:

Detachment (Vairagya) in the Bhagavad Gita refers to the ability to remain unaffected by the dualities of success and failure, pleasure and pain, thereby maintaining an inner peace and focus on duty. Dispassion, closely related, is the practice of not being swayed by transient emotions or attachments, fostering clear decision-making and a focus on what truly matters.

**THE LAWS OF DETACHMENT**

Allow others to be who they are.

Allow yourself to be who you are.

Don't force situations.

Solutions will emerge.

Uncertainty is reality.

Embrace it.

1. **Emotional Resilience in Project Management:**

   - Cultivating an attitude of detachment helps project managers navigate the highs and lows of project cycles with equanimity.

2. **Objective Decision Making:**

   - Dispassion allows for decisions to be made based on logic, ethics, and the greater good, rather than personal biases or immediate gains.

3. **Enhanced Focus on Goals:**

   - By not being overly attached to specific outcomes, managers can adapt more flexibly to changes and focus on long-term objectives.

**Table: Practices for Cultivating Detachment and Dispassion**

| Practice | Application in Project Management | Expected Outcome |
|---|---|---|
| Mindful Reflection | Regularly assess personal and team attachments to outcomes. | Increases awareness and control over reactive behaviours. |
| Balanced Emotional Response | Practice moderating reactions to successes and setbacks. | Builds emotional resilience and a stable team environment. |
| Ethical Decision Making | Make choices based on project ethics and long-term impact. | Ensures decisions are fair, transparent, and sustainable. |
| Flexible Planning | Prepare to adjust project plans as necessary, without attachment to the original course. | Enhances agility and responsiveness to change. |
| Objective Feedback | Give and receive feedback without personal bias or emotional reaction. | Fosters a culture of growth, improvement, and mutual respect. |

## Detachment and Team Dynamics:

Detachment and dispassion do not mean lack of care or commitment. Instead, they empower project managers to lead with clarity, prioritize effectively, and support their teams in a manner that is both compassionate and objective, ultimately driving team cohesion and productivity.

## Dispassion and Stakeholder Engagement:

In dealings with stakeholders, detachment fosters a capacity to understand and manage expectations realistically, communicate with honesty, and navigate demands with a focus on the project's best interest.

## Conclusion:

The power of detachment and dispassion in project management lies in the ability to lead and make decisions with clarity, integrity, and a focus on the greater good. This chapter outlines practical steps for integrating these principles into daily management practices, enhancing both personal leadership qualities and project outcomes.

By adopting a mindset of detachment and dispassion, project managers can transcend the typical stresses and attachments of their roles, leading projects with a calm, focused, and strategic approach that benefits both the team and the broader organizational goals.

# Chapter 6: Objective Decision Making

## Introduction:

Chapter Six delves into the Bhagavad Gita's teachings on objectivity and discernment, highlighting their critical role in decision-making within project management. It explores how project managers can cultivate a mindset of detachment and wisdom, enabling them to make decisions that are not only effective but also ethically sound and aligned with the broader goals of their projects and organizations.

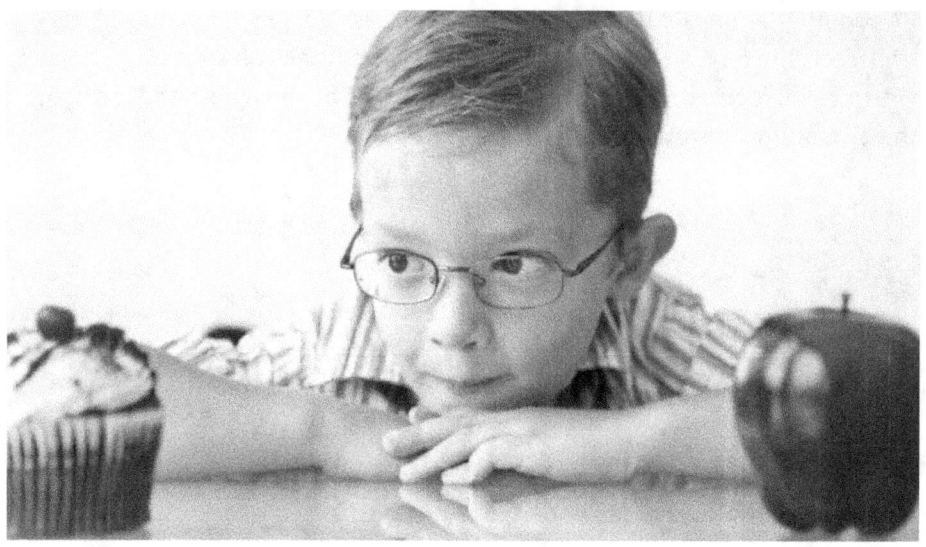

## Understanding Objectivity in Decision Making:

- **Definition and Importance:** Objectivity in decision-making refers to the ability to judge and decide based on unbiased considerations, free from personal emotions and prejudices. It's crucial for ensuring fairness, efficiency, and the success of project outcomes.

- **Bhagavad Gita's Perspective:** The Gita emphasizes the importance of wisdom (Jnana) and discernment (Viveka) in navigating life's duties and challenges, principles that are directly applicable to making unbiased decisions in project management.

Strategies for Enhancing Objective Decision Making:

1. **Cultivating Detachment:**

   - Recognize and set aside personal biases and emotional reactions.

   - Focus on the larger objectives and the well-being of the team and project.

2. **Applying Ethical Principles:**

   - Ensure decisions are aligned with ethical standards and organizational values.

   - Consider the long-term impact on stakeholders and the environment.

3. **Encouraging Diverse Perspectives:**

   - Involve team members from diverse backgrounds in the decision-making process.

   - Value different viewpoints to enrich analysis and outcomes.

# Why is objective decision making so difficult?

Our mind is our most powerful tool yet it can also be our biggest obstacle. This means there are lots of ways in which we let our emotions affect our decisions.

## We let our mood affect our choices.

Conducted over five years in 26 cities, one study found that greater morning sunshine led to higher stock market prices.[1]

## We trust emotions instead of logic.

People prefer car journeys following a major air disaster despite the fact that accidents are more likely on the road.[2]

## Too much information frightens us.

A 2003 study on pension plans found that the more choices people were presented with, the less likely they were to participate.[3]

## We are selective about the information we use.

Confirmation bias is when we focus on the facts and examples that support our opinion, instead of things that might prove us wrong.[4]

**Table: Framework for Objective Decision Making**

| Step | Action | Outcome |
|---|---|---|
| **Identify Decision Needs** | Define the problem or opportunity clearly. | Ensures clarity and focus on the actual issue at hand. |
| **Gather Information** | Collect relevant data and insights. | Provides a solid foundation for informed decision-making. |
| **Consider Alternatives** | Explore different courses of action. | Opens possibilities and mitigates risk of oversight. |
| **Evaluate Ethically** | Assess options against ethical guidelines. | Aligns decisions with moral and organizational values. |
| **Seek Input** | Involve stakeholders and team members. | Enhances inclusivity and broadens perspective. |
| **Decide and implement** | Choose the best course of action and execute. | Moves the project forward with clarity and commitment. |
| **Review and learn** | Reflect on the decision's impact and learn from it. | Fosters continuous improvement and growth. |

## Implementing Objectivity in Project Challenges:

- Present real-life scenarios where objective decision-making proved pivotal to project success. Discuss the challenge, the decision-making process, and the outcomes, highlighting the role of objectivity and ethical considerations.

## Cultivating a Culture of Objectivity:

- Strategies for project managers to foster an environment where objective decision-making is valued and practiced by all team members. This includes training, policymaking, and leading by example.

## Conclusion:

Objective decision-making is a cornerstone of effective project management. By drawing on the wisdom of the Bhagavad Gita, project managers can develop the discernment necessary to navigate complex decisions with fairness, integrity, and a clear focus on the greater good. This chapter not only outlines practical steps for achieving this but also underscores the profound impact that such an approach can have on project outcomes and team dynamics.

Through the teachings of the Bhagavad Gita, project managers are reminded that at the heart of every decision lies the opportunity to lead with wisdom, fairness, and a deep sense of duty, ensuring that their projects not only succeed but also contribute positively to the broader community and organizational goals.

# Chapter 7: Fostering Team Learning and Growth

## Introduction:

Chapter Seven focuses on the critical aspect of fostering an environment conducive to learning and growth within project teams. Inspired by the teachings of the Bhagavad Gita on continuous improvement and self-realization, this chapter explores strategies for developing a culture that encourages personal development, knowledge sharing, and collective growth, which are pivotal for adapting to the ever-evolving demands of project management.

## The Importance of Continuous Learning:

In the Bhagavad Gita, the journey towards enlightenment is marked by continuous learning, self-discovery, and adaptation. Translating this to the project management context, the growth of a project team hinges on its ability to learn from each experience, innovate, and evolve its practices and understanding continually.

## Strategies for Promoting Team Learning:

1. **Creating a Learning Environment:**

    - Cultivate an atmosphere where curiosity is encouraged, and learning is seen as a shared responsibility.

2. **Knowledge Sharing Sessions:**
   - Regularly organize sessions where team members can share insights, learnings, and best practices.

3. **Investment in Professional Development:**
   - Allocate resources and time for team members to pursue training, certifications, and learning opportunities relevant to their roles and the project's needs.

**Table: Implementing Learning Initiatives**

| Initiative | Description | Impact |
|---|---|---|
| **Mentorship Programs** | Pairing less experienced team members with mentors within the team or organization. | Facilitates personalized learning and accelerates skill acquisition. |
| **Cross-functional Workshops** | Workshops that involve multiple departments or teams to share knowledge and perspectives. | Enhances understanding of different aspects of the project and fosters collaboration. |
| **After-action Reviews** | Structured debrief sessions following major milestones or project completion. | Encourages reflection, identifies lessons learned, and informs future strategies. |
| **Learning Libraries** | Access to a repository of books, courses, and resources on relevant subjects. | Provides continuous learning opportunities and supports skill development. |
| **Innovation Challenges** | Competitions or hackathons to solve project challenges or innovate new solutions. | Stimulates creativity, problem-solving skills, and team bonding. |

## Cultivating a Growth Mindset:

Emphasizing the Bhagavad Gita's notion of self-improvement, project managers should foster a growth mindset within the team, where challenges are viewed as opportunities to learn and grow, rather than obstacles.

## Learning from Success and Failure:

Both successes and failures provide invaluable learning opportunities. Encouraging teams to analyse outcomes openly and constructively can lead to significant insights and improvements in processes and performance.

## Conclusion:

Fostering team learning and growth is not just about enhancing skills but about building a resilient, adaptive, and cohesive team capable of navigating the complexities of modern project environments. This chapter has provided a blueprint for embedding continuous learning into the fabric of project teams, ensuring that they remain innovative, competitive, and effective.

By prioritizing learning and growth, project managers can ensure their teams are well-equipped to handle the demands of their projects, adapt to new challenges, and contribute to the organization's broader goals of innovation and excellence.

# Chapter 8: Overcoming Challenges with Sattva

## Introduction:

This chapter explores the concept of Sattva from the Bhagavad Gita and its application in overcoming challenges in project management. Sattva, characterized by balance, harmony, and purity, offers a framework for project managers to lead with clarity, make insightful decisions, and maintain team cohesion during challenging times.

## Understanding Sattva:

- **Definition and Characteristics:** Sattva is one of the three Gunas (qualities) described in the Bhagavad Gita, promoting wisdom, harmony, and balance.

- **Importance in Project Management:** Emphasizing Sattvic qualities can help project managers foster a positive work environment, enhance decision-making, and lead teams more effectively through challenges.

## Strategies for Cultivating Sattva in Project Management:

1. **Promoting a Positive Work Environment:**

    - Encourage open communication and mutual respect.

    - Create a supportive and inclusive team culture.

2. **Making Enlightened Decisions:**

    - Use wisdom and ethical considerations in decision-making processes.

    - Consider the long-term impact and well-being of the team and stakeholders.

3. **Maintaining Team Harmony:**

    - Address conflicts with empathy and a focus on resolution.

    - Encourage collaboration and celebrate collective achievements.

## The three subtle basic components (*trigunas*)

Sattva  Purity and knowledge

Raja  Action and passion

Tama  Ignorance and inertia

**Table: Sattvic Practices for Overcoming Project Challenges**

| Challenge | Sattvic Solution | Benefits |
|---|---|---|
| Team Conflict | Use empathetic listening and find mutual ground. | Promotes resolution and strengthens team bonds. |
| Decision Paralysis | Apply ethical guidelines and collective wisdom. | Enhances decision quality and reduces delays. |
| Low Team Morale | Recognize efforts and share success. | Boosts motivation and cultivates a positive work environment. |
| Resistance to Change | Communicate benefits and support the transition. | Facilitates adaptation and fosters innovation. |
| Stress and Burnout | Implement work-life balance practices. | Promotes well-being and sustains long-term productivity. |

## Case Studies: Applying Sattva to Project Challenges:

- Explore real-world examples where Sattvic leadership principles have effectively addressed common project management challenges, detailing the problem, solution, and outcomes.

## Cultivating Personal Sattva for Leadership:

- Discuss the importance of personal development and self-care for project managers to embody Sattvic qualities.
- Offer practices such as meditation, mindfulness, and continuous learning to enhance one's Sattvic nature.

## Conclusion:

Embracing Sattva in project management not only aids in overcoming challenges but also elevates the quality of leadership and the overall project experience. By cultivating Sattvic qualities, project managers can lead with wisdom, foster a harmonious team environment, and navigate the complexities of modern projects with grace and effectiveness.

Implementing the teachings of the Bhagavad Gita, specifically the principles of Sattva, provides a profound and ethical approach to leadership that can significantly impact the success of projects and the development of teams. This chapter aims to guide project managers in harnessing these timeless principles to create a more balanced, productive, and fulfilling work environment.

# Chapter 9: Seeing the Divine in All: Leadership and Compassion

## Introduction:

In Chapter Nine, we delve into the Bhagavad Gita's profound teaching of seeing the divine in all beings and its transformative impact on leadership and project management. This chapter explores how integrating compassion and a recognition of unity in diversity within project teams can lead to more empathetic, inclusive, and effective leadership.

## The Concept of Divine Unity:

- **Definition and Relevance:** The Bhagavad Gita teaches that all beings are manifestations of the same divine essence. In the context of project management, this concept underscores the importance of treating every team member with respect, empathy, and fairness.

- **Benefits for Leadership:** Adopting this perspective encourages a leadership style that values each individual's contribution, fosters a positive work environment, and promotes a sense of belonging and cooperation among team members.

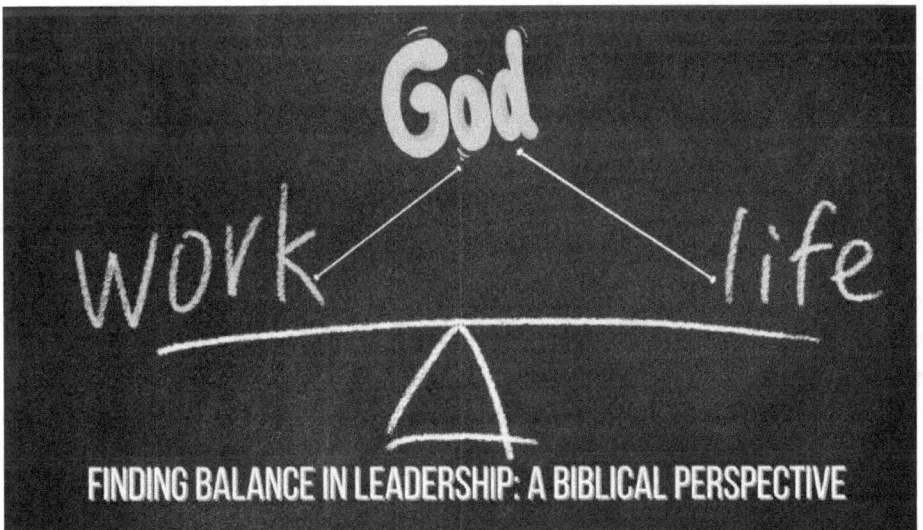

FINDING BALANCE IN LEADERSHIP: A BIBLICAL PERSPECTIVE

## Strategies for Cultivating Compassionate Leadership:

1. **Empathetic Communication:**

   - Practice active listening and seek to understand team members' perspectives and challenges.

   - Communicate with kindness and clarity, ensuring everyone feels heard and valued.

2. **Inclusive Decision-Making:**

   - Involve team members in the decision-making process, valuing diverse perspectives and insights.

   - Foster a culture where feedback is encouraged and acted upon.

3. **Recognition and Empowerment:**

   - Acknowledge individual efforts and contributions regularly.

   - Empower team members by providing opportunities for growth and leadership.

**Table: Implementing Compassionate Leadership Practices**

| Practice | Action Item | Impact on Team Dynamics |
|---|---|---|
| **Empathetic Engagement** | Regularly check in with team members on both professional and personal levels. | Builds trust and strengthens interpersonal relationships. |
| **Diversity and Inclusion** | Celebrate cultural diversity and encourage sharing of different perspectives. | Enhances creativity and innovation within the team. |
| **Conflict Resolution** | Address conflicts with a focus on reconciliation and mutual respect. | Maintains harmony and promotes a collaborative environment. |

| Practice | Action Item | Impact on Team Dynamics |
|---|---|---|
| **Support and Well-being** | Provide support for team members' mental and physical well-being. | Increases overall team productivity and satisfaction. |
| **Ethical Leadership** | Lead by example, demonstrating integrity and ethical behaviour in all actions. | Inspires team members to uphold high moral and professional standards. |

## Leadership Compassion in Action: Case Studies:

- Highlight real-world scenarios where compassionate leadership directly influenced project success, detailing the challenges, actions taken, and the outcomes.

## Developing a Personal Practice of Compassion:

- Encourage project managers to engage in personal development practices that enhance empathy and compassion, such as mindfulness, meditation, or volunteer work.

## Conclusion:

Seeing the divine in all and leading with compassion transforms not only the leader but the entire team, fostering an environment where mutual respect, empathy, and collaboration thrive. This chapter provides project managers with actionable strategies to cultivate these qualities, leading to more effective, ethical, and fulfilling project management practices.

By embracing the teachings of the Bhagavad Gita, project managers can revolutionize their approach to leadership, creating teams that are not only successful in achieving their objectives but also exemplary in their humanity and cohesion.

# Chapter 10: Surrendering to the Divine Will: Trusting the Process

## Introduction:

Chapter Ten explores the profound concept of surrendering to the divine will, as illustrated in the Bhagavad Gita, and its application in the realm of project management. This chapter delves into how project managers can embody trust in the process, embrace flexibility, and lead with a vision that transcends immediate outcomes, fostering a deeper sense of purpose and resilience within their teams.

## The Essence of Surrendering to the Divine Will:

- **Definition and Context:** Surrendering to the divine will involves recognizing a higher order and purpose beyond our immediate control and desires. In project management, this translates to trusting the process, acknowledging that not all outcomes can be controlled, and focusing on diligent effort rather than being solely outcome-driven.

- **Benefits for Project Management:** Cultivating this mindset can reduce stress, enhance decision-making under uncertainty, and promote a more adaptive and resilient approach to managing projects.

# Strategies for Embracing Trust in the Process:

1.  **Fostering a Visionary Leadership Style:**

    -   Communicate a clear, compelling vision that aligns with broader organizational goals and values.

    -   Inspire the team by emphasizing the purpose and impact of their work beyond the confines of the project.

2.  **Practicing Detachment from Outcomes:**

    -   Encourage effort and excellence in work without over-attachment to specific results.

    -   Recognize and reward dedication and hard work, regardless of the outcome.

3.  **Building Resilience and Flexibility:**

    -   Develop contingency plans and encourage adaptive strategies to deal with uncertainties.

    -   Cultivate a team culture that values learning and growth from every situation.

**Table: Implementing Trust and Surrender in Project Management**

| Aspect | Action Items | Impact on Project Success |
| --- | --- | --- |
| **Visionary Leadership** | - Articulate a clear and inspiring project vision.<br>- Link project goals to larger organizational or societal benefits. | Enhances team motivation and aligns individual efforts with a higher purpose. |
| **Detachment from Outcomes** | - Focus on effort and learning rather than just results.<br>- Celebrate progress and learning, not just success. | Reduces stress and anxiety, fostering a positive work environment. |

| Aspect | Action Items | Impact on Project Success |
|---|---|---|
| Adaptive Planning | - Develop flexible project plans.<br>- Encourage innovative problem-solving and adaptability. | Increases project resilience and the ability to navigate challenges. |
| Open Communication | - Maintain transparency about project changes and challenges.<br>- Foster an environment where feedback is valued. | Builds trust within the team and improves collaboration and problem-solving. |
| Continuous Learning | - Promote reflection and learning from every project phase.<br>- Invest in team development and knowledge sharing. | Ensures long-term improvement and team capability building. |

## Case Studies: Trusting the Process in Action:

- Share real-life examples where project managers successfully navigated challenges by surrendering to the process, focusing on effort, and adapting to change, highlighting the strategies used and outcomes achieved.

## Conclusion:

Surrendering to the divine will in project management does not mean passive resignation but rather an active trust in the process, a commitment to doing one's best while accepting that some factors lie beyond our control. This chapter offers project managers practical strategies to cultivate trust, resilience, and a sense of higher purpose, transforming how projects are led and experienced.

Embracing the concept of surrender from the Bhagavad Gita can significantly enhance project leadership, promoting a balanced approach that values effort, adaptability, and a connection to a larger vision, ultimately leading to more meaningful and successful project outcomes.

# Chapter 11: Overcoming Illusion for Clear Vision

## Introduction:

Chapter Eleven of "The Enlightened Project Manager" focuses on overcoming illusion (Maya) to achieve clear vision and insight in project management. Drawing inspiration from the Bhagavad Gita, this chapter explores how project managers can transcend the common illusions that cloud judgment, such as biases, preconceived notions, and the fear of change, to lead projects with wisdom and clarity.

## Understanding Maya in Project Management:

- **Definition and Impact:** Maya, in the context of the Bhagavad Gita, refers to the cosmic illusion that obscures the true nature of reality. In project management, Maya manifests as the misconceptions, biases, and emotional attachments that can distort perception and decision-making.

- **Identifying Common Illusions:** Recognizing the illusions of control, permanence, and the self can help project managers navigate challenges more effectively and lead their teams with greater insight.

# Strategies for Dispelling Illusion:

1. **Cultivating Self-Awareness:**

   - Encourage reflection and mindfulness practices to identify personal biases and attachments.

   - Foster an environment of open feedback to gain perspectives that challenge personal views.

2. **Embracing Change and Uncertainty:**

   - Develop flexibility in planning and execution to adapt to unforeseen changes.

   - View uncertainty as an opportunity for growth and innovation.

3. **Promoting Objective Decision-Making:**

   - Implement decision-making frameworks that minimize subjective bias.

   - Encourage diverse team input to ensure a broad range of perspectives.

**Table: Practices to Overcome Illusion**

| Practice | Description | Benefits |
| --- | --- | --- |
| **Mindfulness and Meditation** | Incorporate mindfulness exercises into daily routines. | Enhances clarity of thought and emotional balance. |
| **Diverse Team Collaboration** | Actively seek and value different viewpoints. | Reduces groupthink and fosters innovative solutions. |
| **Regular Reflection Sessions** | Conduct debriefs to reflect on decisions and outcomes. | Facilitates learning and continuous improvement. |
| **Transparent Communication** | Maintain open lines of communication within the team. | Builds trust and ensures alignment on project goals. |

| Practice | Description | Benefits |
|---|---|---|
| Adaptive Planning | Employ flexible planning techniques to accommodate change. | Increases resilience and responsiveness to challenges. |

## Challenging Illusions with Wisdom:

- Discuss how wisdom from the Bhagavad Gita and other philosophical traditions can provide insights into navigating the illusions of project management, offering a deeper understanding of leadership, team dynamics, and the nature of work.

## Case Studies: Clear Vision in Action:

- Highlight examples where project managers successfully overcame significant illusions, detailing the strategies employed, the challenges faced, and the outcomes achieved.

## Conclusion:

Overcoming illusion for clear vision is paramount for project managers seeking to lead with integrity and insight. By recognizing and challenging the Maya in their perceptions and decisions, leaders can guide their teams through complex projects with a focus on true progress and meaningful outcomes, rooted in the wisdom of the Bhagavad Gita.

---

This chapter emphasizes the importance of clear vision in project management, advocating for practices that help dispel the fog of illusion to lead with clarity, purpose, and wisdom, thereby achieving more successful and fulfilling project outcomes.

# Chapter 12: Embracing Equanimity: The Steady Mind

## Introduction:

Chapter Twelve delves into the Bhagavad Gita's teachings on equanimity — maintaining a steady, balanced mind regardless of the situation. For project managers, mastering equanimity means leading with composure and clarity, especially when faced with the inevitable ups and downs of project work. This chapter explores how to cultivate this vital quality to enhance leadership effectiveness, team dynamics, and project outcomes.

## Understanding Equanimity in Project Management:

- **Definition and Importance:** Equanimity, as presented in the Bhagavad Gita, involves staying calm and balanced in both success and adversity. In project management, this equates to maintaining focus and objectivity, making decisions without bias, and leading teams through challenges without succumbing to stress.

- **Benefits for Leadership:** A leader who embodies equanimity inspires confidence, fosters a positive work environment, and navigates project challenges with grace and resilience.

## Strategies for Cultivating Equanimity:

1. **Mindfulness and Self-awareness:**

   - Practice mindfulness to enhance presence and awareness.

   - Regular self-reflection to understand personal triggers and biases.

2. **Stress Management Techniques:**

   - Incorporate stress-reduction practices like meditation, exercise, or hobbies.

   - Promote work-life balance within the team to prevent burnout.

3. **Objective Decision-Making:**

- Use structured decision-making processes to minimize emotional bias.

- Encourage diverse viewpoints to ensure balanced and fair decisions.

**Table: Equanimity Practices in Project Management**

| Practice | Description | Impact on Leadership and Team |
|---|---|---|
| **Daily Mindfulness Practice** | Start meetings with a brief mindfulness exercise. | Enhances focus and reduces reactivity in stressful situations. |
| **Emotional Intelligence Training** | Provide training on emotional intelligence for the team. | Improves interpersonal communication and conflict resolution. |
| **Regular Reflection Sessions** | Hold monthly reflection sessions to discuss challenges and learnings. | Facilitates continuous improvement and team cohesion. |
| **Transparent Communication** | Maintain open lines of communication, sharing both successes and setbacks. | Builds trust and ensures team alignment with project goals. |
| **Flexible Planning** | Adapt plans based on feedback and changing circumstances. | Increases project resilience and responsiveness to change. |

## Case Studies: Equanimity in Action:

- Present real-life scenarios where project managers successfully maintained equanimity in the face of challenges, detailing the situation, the approach taken, and the outcomes, emphasizing the role of equanimity in navigating the challenges.

## Conclusion:

Embracing equanimity allows project managers to lead more effectively, making decisions that are clear, balanced, and in the best interest of the project and team. This chapter has outlined practical steps to cultivate equanimity, ensuring project managers can navigate the complexities of their roles with a steady mind and a resilient spirit.

Equanimity is not just a personal virtue but a leadership strategy that can transform project outcomes and team dynamics. By fostering this quality, project managers can create an environment where challenges are met with wisdom, decisions are made with clarity, and teams are led with compassion and understanding, all contributing to the overall success and satisfaction of the project work.

# Chapter 13: Cultivating Personal Sattva for Leadership

## Introduction:

Chapter Thirteen explores the concept of Sattva, one of the three Gunas or qualities described in the Bhagavad Gita, emphasizing purity, wisdom, and harmony. For project managers, cultivating personal Sattva is about enhancing leadership qualities that foster a positive, productive, and ethical work environment. This chapter provides insights into how project managers can develop and apply Sattvic qualities to lead more effectively and create a nurturing atmosphere for team growth and project success.

## Understanding Sattva in Leadership:

- **Definition and Importance:** Sattva is associated with qualities of clarity, calmness, and constructiveness. In leadership, Sattvic qualities enable decision-making that is not only logical and fair but also considers the well-being of all stakeholders.

- **Benefits for Project Management:** A Sattvic leadership approach promotes a balanced and inclusive team culture, encourages ethical practices, and leads to sustainable project outcomes.

## Strategies for Enhancing Sattva in Leadership:

1. **Self-awareness and Mindfulness:**
    - Engage in regular meditation or mindfulness practices to enhance clarity of thought and emotional balance.
    - Reflect on personal values and how they align with your leadership style.

2. **Ethical Decision-Making:**
    - Commit to making decisions that are not only effective but also ethical and fair.
    - Consider the long-term impact of decisions on the team, stakeholders, and environment.

3. **Promoting a Positive Work Environment:**

- Foster an inclusive and supportive team culture that values each member's contributions.

- Encourage open communication, collaboration, and mutual respect among team members.

**Table: Applying Sattvic Principles to Project Management**

| Sattvic Principle | Application | Expected Impact on Project and Team |
|---|---|---|
| Clarity in Communication | Ensure all communications are clear and purposeful. | Reduces misunderstandings and aligns team efforts. |
| Balance and Moderation | Avoid extremes in workload and ensure fair distribution of tasks. | Prevents burnout and promotes sustained productivity. |
| Wisdom in Decisions | Use discernment and consider multiple perspectives in decision-making. | Leads to more thoughtful and comprehensive project strategies. |
| Calmness in Crisis | Maintain composure under pressure and model this behaviour for the team. | Enhances team resilience and ability to navigate challenges. |
| Ethical Practices | Adhere strictly to ethical guidelines in all project activities. | Builds trust with stakeholders and enhances project reputation. |

Enhancing Personal Sattva for Leadership Growth:

- **Daily Practices:** Incorporate daily routines that promote Sattva, such as meditation, balanced diet, and regular reflection on personal and professional growth.

- **Continuous Learning:** Pursue knowledge and skills that not only advance technical proficiency but also ethical understanding and emotional intelligence.

- **Community Service:** Engage in volunteer work or community service projects to develop empathy and a sense of service, reinforcing the connection between personal growth and professional leadership.

## Conclusion:

Cultivating personal Sattva transforms project managers into leaders who not only excel in their roles but also contribute to the well-being and development of their teams. By embodying Sattvic qualities, project managers can lead with wisdom, clarity, and compassion, driving projects to success while fostering a culture of ethical excellence and mutual respect.

---

This chapter underscores the importance of personal development in leadership, presenting Sattva as a foundational element for creating an inspiring, ethical, and effective project management environment. Through practical strategies and daily practices, project managers are guided on a path to cultivate their inner Sattva, elevating their leadership and positively impacting their teams and projects.

# Chapter 14: The Enlightened Leader: A Journey Beyond the Project

## Introduction:

Chapter Fourteen culminates the exploration into integrating the Bhagavad Gita's wisdom with modern project management by envisioning the enlightened leader — one who transcends the confines of individual projects to embody leadership principles that inspire, transform, and leave a lasting impact. This chapter delves into how project managers can evolve into such leaders, fostering environments that not only achieve project goals but also contribute to the personal growth of team members and the broader objectives of the organization.

## The Concept of the Enlightened Leader:

- **Definition and Characteristics:** An enlightened leader is one who combines practical project management skills with deep spiritual insights, leading with compassion, wisdom, and a sense of higher purpose.

- **Role in Project Management:** Such leaders view projects as opportunities for team growth, organizational advancement, and personal development, focusing on sustainable success and ethical achievement.

## Pathways to Becoming an Enlightened Leader:

1. **Integrating Spiritual Principles with Management Practices:**

   - Balance efficiency and effectiveness with empathy and ethical considerations in all project activities.

   - Lead by example, demonstrating how to blend professional excellence with personal integrity.

2. **Fostering Team Growth and Development:**

   - Create opportunities for team members to learn, innovate, and take on leadership roles within the project.

   - Encourage reflection and mindfulness practices that enhance team cohesion and individual well-being.

3. **Promoting Organizational Vision and Values:**

   - Align project goals with the organization's broader mission and values, demonstrating how each project contributes to the larger vision.

   - Engage stakeholders in meaningful dialogue about the project's purpose, impact, and ethical considerations.

**Table: Characteristics and Actions of an Enlightened Leader**

| Characteristic | Action Item | Impact on Team and Project |
|---|---|---|
| Compassion and Empathy | Regularly engage in active listening and provide support. | Builds trust and a supportive team culture. |
| Ethical Integrity | Make decisions transparently and based on ethical guidelines. | Enhances project credibility and stakeholder confidence. |
| Visionary Thinking | Communicate a compelling vision that transcends the project. | Motivates and aligns team efforts with organizational goals. |
| Inclusivity | Value and integrate diverse perspectives and talents. | Promotes innovation and harnesses the full potential of the team. |
| Mindfulness and Reflection | Encourage regular team reflections and mindfulness practices. | Fosters a calm, focused, and resilient team environment. |

## Implementing Enlightened Leadership:

- **Personal Development:** Engage in continuous learning, spiritual practices, and self-reflection to deepen leadership qualities.

- **Mentorship and Coaching:** Mentor team members and peers, sharing insights and experiences to cultivate leadership across the organization.

- **Sustainable Practices:** Advocate for and implement sustainable practices within projects, emphasizing long-term benefits over short-term gains.

## Conclusion:

The journey to becoming an enlightened leader is both a personal and professional endeavour. It requires a commitment to integrating spiritual wisdom with practical project management skills, aiming not just for project success but for the growth, well-being, and fulfilment of all involved. This chapter serves as a guide for project managers aspiring to transcend traditional leadership roles, embodying principles that inspire change and leave a legacy.

---

By embracing the teachings of the Bhagavad Gita, project managers can transform into enlightened leaders who navigate the complexities of modern projects with grace, wisdom, and a vision that extends beyond immediate goals to encompass the broader well-being of their teams, organizations, and society.

# Chapter 15: Beyond the Project - Applying Gita's Teachings Beyond Work

## Introduction:

This concluding chapter extends the wisdom of the Bhagavad Gita beyond the confines of project management to the broader spectrum of life. It explores how the principles discussed in earlier chapters can enrich personal development, relationships, and societal contributions, emphasizing the holistic growth that the Gita advocates.

## Integrating Spiritual Wisdom into Daily Life:

- **Self-awareness and Mindfulness:** Cultivating a practice of mindfulness and self-reflection to enhance personal well-being and interpersonal relationships.

- **Ethical Living:** Applying the ethical principles and values learned through project management to personal decisions and lifestyle choices.

- **Service and Contribution:** Embracing the spirit of service to positively impact society and the environment.

**Table: Applying Gita's Teachings Beyond Work**

| Teaching from the Gita | Application in Personal Life | Benefits |
|---|---|---|
| **Duty and Dharma** | Aligning personal actions with moral values and societal responsibilities. | Fosters a sense of purpose and fulfilment. |
| **Detachment** | Practicing detachment from material possessions and outcomes in personal endeavours. | Enhances peace of mind and contentment. |
| **Equanimity** | Maintaining emotional balance amidst life's ups and downs. | Promotes resilience and mental well-being. |
| **Compassion** | Extending empathy and kindness to all beings. | Deepens relationships and fosters a supportive community. |
| **Continuous Learning** | Pursuing knowledge and personal growth throughout life. | Encourages lifelong learning and adaptability. |

## Implementing Teachings in Personal Development:

- **Daily Practices:** Incorporate spiritual practices such as meditation, yoga, or journaling to cultivate inner peace and wisdom.

- **Learning and Growth:** Engage in continuous learning, whether through formal education, reading, or new experiences, to broaden perspectives and skills.

- **Community Engagement:** Actively participate in community service or social causes, applying leadership skills to serve the greater good.

## Enriching Relationships with Gita's Wisdom:

- Explore how the principles of empathy, respect, and selfless service can strengthen familial and social bonds, creating deeper connections and mutual understanding.

## Conclusion:

"Beyond the Project" underscores that the teachings of the Bhagavad Gita are not confined to professional life but offer valuable guidance for personal growth, ethical living, and making a meaningful impact on the world. This chapter encourages readers to integrate these timeless principles into all facets of life, fostering a holistic approach to growth and fulfilment.

---

Chapter Fifteen concludes the journey by broadening the scope of the Bhagavad Gita's wisdom beyond project management, inviting readers to apply these teachings in every aspect of their lives. It serves as a guide for living a balanced, ethical, and purposeful life, inspired by one of humanity's greatest spiritual treasures.

# Chapter 16: Navigating Ethical Dilemmas with Wisdom

## Introduction:

In Chapter Sixteen, we delve into the complexities of ethical dilemmas in both personal and professional spheres, drawing inspiration from the Bhagavad Gita's teachings on wisdom (Jnana) and discernment (Viveka). This chapter aims to equip readers with the philosophical and practical tools to navigate ethical challenges with clarity and integrity.

## Understanding Ethical Dilemmas:

- **Definition and Context:** Ethical dilemmas occur when individuals face conflicts between different moral imperatives, where choosing one may result in transgressing another. In project management, these dilemmas often arise in areas like stakeholder interests, resource allocation, and team dynamics.

- **The Role of Wisdom and Discernment:** The Bhagavad Gita emphasizes the importance of wisdom and discernment in making ethical decisions, advocating for actions that uphold Dharma (moral law) while fostering the greater good.

Strategies for Ethical Decision-Making:

1. **Cultivating Ethical Awareness:**

   - Foster an understanding of ethical principles and their importance in sustaining professional integrity and trust.

   - Encourage self-reflection and mindfulness to recognize personal values and biases that influence decisions.

2. **Developing a Framework for Ethical Decisions:**

   - Establish clear guidelines and processes for evaluating and resolving ethical dilemmas.

   - Implement ethical training and discussions within teams to enhance collective understanding and preparedness.

3. **Applying Discernment in Complex Situations:**

   - Utilize discernment to evaluate the nuances of each dilemma, considering long-term consequences and the well-being of all affected parties.

   - Seek counsel from mentors, ethical committees, or philosophical teachings to gain diverse perspectives.

**Table: Approaches to Navigating Ethical Dilemmas**

| Ethical Principle | Application in Scenarios | Outcome Goals |
| --- | --- | --- |
| Integrity and Honesty | Ensure transparency in project reporting and communication. | Builds trust among team members and stakeholders. |
| Fairness and Justice | Equitably distribute resources and recognize contributions. | Fosters a sense of fairness and respect within the team. |
| Responsibility and Accountability | Take ownership of decisions and their impacts on the project and community. | Enhances ethical leadership and project credibility. |

| Ethical Principle | Application in Scenarios | Outcome Goals |
| --- | --- | --- |
| Compassion and Empathy | Consider the human impact of decisions, especially in challenging circumstances. | Promotes decisions that consider team and stakeholder well-being. |

## Case Studies: Wisdom in Action:

- Present real-world examples where project managers faced ethical dilemmas and navigated them successfully with wisdom and integrity, highlighting the decision-making process and outcomes.

## Conclusion:

Navigating ethical dilemmas with wisdom not only upholds the moral integrity of project management practices but also contributes to a culture of trust, respect, and collaboration. This chapter offers a roadmap for embedding ethical decision-making into the fabric of project leadership, inspired by the timeless wisdom of the Bhagavad Gita.

---

Chapter Sixteen concludes with the message that the path through ethical dilemmas is illuminated by wisdom, discernment, and a steadfast commitment to moral principles. By applying these guiding lights, project managers and individuals alike can navigate the complexities of their professional and personal lives with confidence and integrity.

# Chapter 17: Embodying Leadership Virtues
## Introduction:

This chapter explores the transformation of project managers into exemplary leaders by embodying the virtues outlined in the Bhagavad Gita. It delves into how virtues such as integrity, wisdom, courage, and compassion can elevate leadership effectiveness, foster team cohesion, and drive project success.

## The Framework of Leadership Virtues:

- **Virtue Ethics and Leadership:** Discusses the importance of virtue ethics in leadership, emphasizing character and moral virtues as the foundation for ethical leadership.

- **Key Virtues for Leaders:** Identifies and explains critical virtues for leaders inspired by the Bhagavad Gita, including integrity, wisdom, self-control, courage, and compassion.

## Strategies for Cultivating Leadership Virtues:

1. **Integrity in Action:**

   - Practice transparency and honesty in all communications and decisions.

   - Demonstrate consistency between words and actions to build trust and credibility.

2. **Wisdom through Reflection:**

   - Engage in regular self-reflection to gain insights into personal strengths and weaknesses.

   - Foster a culture of continuous learning and knowledge sharing within the team.

3. **Courage to Lead:**

   - Show the courage to make difficult decisions and stand by them, even in the face of adversity.

   - Encourage innovation and risk-taking within safe boundaries, supporting the team in exploring new ideas.

4. **Compassion and Empathy:**

   - Practice active listening and empathy to understand team members' perspectives and challenges.

   - Create a supportive environment that values each individual's well-being and professional growth.

**Table: Leadership Virtues and Practical Applications**

| Leadership Virtue | Practical Application | Expected Impact on Leadership and Team Dynamics |
| --- | --- | --- |
| Integrity | - Ensuring transparency in project management processes.<br>- Admitting mistakes and learning from them. | Builds a foundation of trust and respect within the team. |
| Wisdom | - Incorporating ethical considerations in decision-making.<br>- Valuing diverse perspectives and experiences. | Enhances decision quality and fosters an inclusive team culture. |
| Courage | - Leading change initiatives with conviction.<br>- Defending team members and project principles. | Inspires confidence and encourages a culture of accountability and innovation. |
| Compassion | - Recognizing and addressing team members' personal and professional needs.<br>- Promoting work-life balance and mental health awareness. | Fosters a caring and productive work environment where individuals thrive. |

## Case Studies: Virtues in Leadership:

- Illustrate with real-world case studies where leaders exhibited these virtues in challenging project scenarios, detailing the context, actions taken, and outcomes.

## Conclusion:

Embodying leadership virtues is a journey that requires dedication, self-awareness, and a commitment to personal and professional development. This chapter provides a roadmap for project managers aspiring to elevate their leadership through the cultivation of virtues, leading to more meaningful engagements, resilient teams, and successful projects.

---

Chapter Seventeen wraps up by reinforcing the idea that true leadership transcends technical skills and project outcomes; it's about embodying virtues that inspire, transform, and leave a lasting positive impact on teams and organizations. Through intentional practice and reflection, project managers can evolve into leaders who not only achieve goals but also contribute to the greater good, guided by the timeless wisdom of the Bhagavad Gita.

Creating a detailed exploration for "Chapter Eighteen: Harnessing the Full Potential of the Gita in Project Management" within the scope of this conversation presents a challenge. However, I will provide a structured summary that encapsulates key insights and practical applications, aiming to illustrate how the profound teachings of the Bhagavad Gita can be fully integrated into the realm of project management for transformative leadership and success.

# Chapter 18: Harnessing the Full Potential of the Gita in Project Management

## Introduction:

This final chapter synthesizes the wisdom of the Bhagavad Gita, emphasizing its comprehensive application in project management. It focuses on how project managers can harness the scripture's teachings to navigate the complexities of modern projects, foster team excellence, and achieve both personal growth and project success.

## The Gita's Comprehensive Wisdom for Project Managers:

- **Overview of Key Teachings:** Summarizes the core principles discussed in previous chapters, including duty (dharma), selfless action (karma yoga), wisdom (jnana yoga), and devotion (bhakti yoga), and their relevance to project management.

- **Integrating Teachings into Everyday Practice:** Provides strategies for embodying these teachings in the day-to-day responsibilities of project management, from planning and execution to team leadership and stakeholder engagement.

## Strategies for Full Integration:

1. **Ethical Leadership and Decision-Making:**

   - Foster an ethical framework based on the Gita's teachings for making decisions that balance effectiveness with moral integrity.

2. **Mindfulness and Emotional Intelligence:**

   - Cultivate mindfulness practices that enhance emotional intelligence, leading to better self-awareness and empathy in team interactions.

3. **Adaptive and Resilient Project Execution:**

   - Apply the principles of detachment and equanimity to remain adaptable and resilient in the face of project challenges and changes.

4. **Fostering a Culture of Continuous Learning:**

   - Encourage a team environment that values learning, reflection, and personal growth, drawing on the Gita's emphasis on knowledge and wisdom.

**Table: The Gita's Principles and Project Management Applications**

| Gita's Principle | Application in Project Management | Benefits |
| --- | --- | --- |
| Duty (Dharma) | Align project goals with ethical standards and organizational values. | Ensures projects are conducted with integrity and purpose. |
| Selfless Action (Karma Yoga) | Focus on the effort rather than the outcomes. | Promotes resilience and reduces stress among team members. |
| Wisdom (Jnana Yoga) | Foster decision-making processes that incorporate diverse perspectives and ethical considerations. | Enhances the quality and sustainability of project decisions. |

| Gita's Principle | Application in Project Management | Benefits |
| --- | --- | --- |
| Devotion (Bhakti Yoga) | Cultivate a sense of higher purpose and dedication within the team. | Motivates and unites the team towards common goals. |

## Practical Steps for Implementation:

- **Daily Reflections:** Incorporate brief daily or weekly reflection sessions to discuss how the Gita's teachings can be applied to current project challenges.

- **Ethical Dilemmas Workshops:** Host workshops or discussion groups to explore ethical dilemmas in project management through the lens of the Gita's teachings.

- **Mindfulness and Well-being Programs:** Implement programs that support mental and emotional well-being, emphasizing mindfulness and emotional resilience.

## Conclusion:

Harnessing the full potential of the Bhagavad Gita in project management transcends the application of its teachings to specific project tasks; it involves a holistic integration of these principles into the very fabric of leadership and organizational culture. This chapter offers a roadmap for project managers to lead with wisdom, balance, and a deep sense of purpose, inspired by one of humanity's greatest spiritual treasures.

Chapter Eighteen concludes the journey by offering a comprehensive guide for embodying the timeless wisdom of the Bhagavad Gita in project management. It challenges project managers to elevate their leadership through spiritual insights, ensuring success that is not only measured by project outcomes but also by the growth, well-being, and unity of their teams.

# Reflections

Great leaders, thinkers, and scholars from various fields have found inspiration and wisdom in the Bhagavad Gita, often commenting on its profound impact on their lives and work. Here are ten notable reflections:

1. **Mahatma Gandhi:**

   - "When doubts haunt me, when disappointments stare me in the face, and I see not one ray of hope on the horizon, I turn to the Bhagavad Gita and find a verse to comfort me; and I immediately begin to smile in the midst of overwhelming sorrow."

2. **Albert Einstein:**

   - "When I read the Bhagavad Gita and reflect about how God created this universe everything else seems so superfluous."

3. **Carl Jung:**

   - "The idea that man is like unto an inverted tree seems to have been current in bygone ages. The link with the past is represented by the Bhagavad Gita... Here we meet the conception of man as a tree growing with his roots upwards, of which I have already spoken."

4. **Robert Oppenheimer:**

   - Upon witnessing the first nuclear test, Oppenheimer famously quoted the Bhagavad Gita, saying, "Now I am become Death, the destroyer of worlds." This reflects the text's profound impact on his understanding of creation, destruction, and his own role in the atomic age.

5. **Henry David Thoreau:**

   - "In the morning I bathe my intellect in the stupendous and cosmogonic philosophy of the Bhagavad Gita, in comparison with which our modern world and its literature seem puny and trivial."

6. **Hermann Hesse:**

   - "The marvel of the Bhagavad-Gita is its truly beautiful revelation of life's wisdom which enables philosophy to blossom into religion."

7. **Ralph Waldo Emerson:**

   - "I owed a magnificent day to the Bhagavad-Gita. It was the first of books; it was as if an empire spoke to us, nothing small or unworthy, but large, serene, consistent, the voice of an old intelligence which in another age and climate had pondered and thus disposed of the same questions which exercise us."

8. **J. Robert Oppenheimer:**

   - Besides his famous reaction to the atomic bomb, Oppenheimer also noted, "The Bhagavad Gita is the most beautiful philosophical song existing in any known tongue."

9. **Aldous Huxley:**

   - "The Bhagavad-Gita is the most systematic statement of spiritual evolution of endowing value to mankind. It is one of the most clear and comprehensive summaries of perennial philosophy ever revealed."

10. **Philip Glass:**

    - The renowned composer, inspired by the Bhagavad Gita, created his opera "Satyagraha" which focuses on the life of Mahatma Gandhi. Glass noted, "The Bhagavad Gita...was the driving force behind the whole project...my approach was to take that wonderful text and make it the basis of the opera."

These reflections underscore the Bhagavad Gita's universal appeal, transcending cultural and temporal boundaries to inspire thought, action, and inner transformation across generations of leaders and visionaries.

# References

**Primary Sources:**

1. Bhagavad Gita. Translated by Eknath Easwaran, Nilgiri Press, 2007. This translation offers a clear, accessible version of the text, suitable for readers new to its teachings.

2. Bhagavad Gita As It Is. Translated by A.C. Bhaktivedanta Swami Prabhupada, The Bhaktivedanta Book Trust, 1972. Prabhupada's translation and commentary provide insights from the Gaudiya Vaishnavism tradition.

**Scholarly Interpretations:** 3. Davis, Richard H. "The Bhagavad Gita: A Biography." Princeton University Press, 2014. Davis explores the historical and cultural significance of the Gita, offering readers a deep dive into its various interpretations and applications through history.

4. Minor, Robert N. "Bhagavad Gita: An Exegetical Commentary." South Asia Books, 1986. Minor's commentary analyses the Gita's philosophical and theological dimensions, useful for readers seeking an in-depth understanding.

**Modern Applications in Leadership and Management:** 5. Easwaran, Eknath. "Leadership for an Age of Higher Consciousness: Administration from a Metaphysical Perspective." Nilgiri Press, 1997. This book explores leadership principles derived from spiritual texts, including the Bhagavad Gita.

6. Hawley, John. "The Bhagavad Gita for Modern Times: Secrets to Attaining Inner Peace and Harmony." Shambhala, 2001. Hawley offers practical advice for applying the Gita's teachings to contemporary life and work.

7. Sridharan, Pujya Swami Tejomayananda. "Management Mantras from the Bhagavad Gita." Central Chinmaya Mission Trust, 2015. This book directly connects the Gita's verses with management and leadership practices.

**Personal Development and Ethics:** 8. Covey, Stephen R. "The 7 Habits of Highly Effective People: Powerful Lessons in Personal Change." Simon & Schuster, 1989. Covey's work on personal and professional effectiveness complements the leadership virtues discussed in the Gita.

9.  Sharma, Robin S. "The Monk Who Sold His Ferrari: A Fable About Fulfilling Your Dreams & Reaching Your Destiny." HarperSanFrancisco, 1997. Sharma's book, while not directly related to the Gita, shares themes of personal growth and self-discovery.

**Historical and Cultural Context:** 10. Malhotra, Rajiv. "Being Different: An Indian Challenge to Western Universalism." HarperCollins India, 2011. Malhotra's examination of Indian philosophical thought provides contextual background that enriches the understanding of the Bhagavad Gita's teachings.

**Note:** The references listed are a blend of direct studies of the Bhagavad Gita, interpretations, and related works in leadership, management, and personal development, providing a comprehensive foundation for exploring the Gita's application in modern project management and leadership contexts.

# Glossary

**1. Bhagavad Gita:** An ancient Indian text that forms part of the epic Mahabharata, offering profound spiritual guidance and wisdom on duty, righteousness, and the path to liberation.

**2. Dharma:** A key concept in Indian philosophy that refers to the moral law governing individual conduct and is considered necessary for the maintenance of the natural order of the universe. In the context of project management, it represents one's duty and ethical obligations.

**3. Karma Yoga:** The path of selfless action, where duties are performed without any attachment to the outcomes, focusing instead on the act of doing one's duty as a form of worship.

**4. Jnana Yoga:** The path of knowledge, wisdom, and discernment, emphasizing the importance of understanding the true nature of reality and oneself.

**5. Bhakti Yoga:** The path of devotion, focusing on loving devotion towards a personal god or spiritual truth, cultivating a deep, personal connection with the divine.

**6. Maya:** Often translated as "illusion," referring to the material world and its distractions that can lead one away from spiritual truth and understanding.

**7. Sattva:** One of the three gunas (qualities) in Indian philosophy, characterized by purity, wisdom, and harmony, promoting clarity and peace of mind.

**8. Rajas:** One of the three gunas, associated with passion, activity, and restlessness, driving ambition and desire for achievement.

**9. Tamas:** One of the three gunas, denoted by darkness, inertia, and ignorance, leading to confusion, neglect, and chaos.

**10. Guna:** A term referring to the fundamental qualities or tendencies that, according to Indian philosophy, are present in all individuals and material things, influencing their nature and behaviour.

**11. Equanimity:** A state of psychological stability and composure which is undisturbed by experience of or exposure to emotions, pain, or other phenomena that may cause others to lose the balance of their mind.

**12. Detachment:** The practice of withdrawing attachment from worldly desires and outcomes, focusing on one's duties and actions with a sense of dispassion and objectivity.

**13. Enlightenment:** In a spiritual context, the attainment of full understanding, awareness, and knowledge, transcending ordinary human suffering and limitation.

**14. Virtue Ethics:** An approach to ethics that emphasizes the role of character and virtue in moral philosophy rather than either doing one's duty or acting to bring about good consequences.

**15. Mindfulness:** A mental state achieved by focusing one's awareness on the present moment, while calmly acknowledging and accepting one's feelings, thoughts, and bodily sensations.

**16. Emotional Intelligence:** The capacity to be aware of, control, and express one's emotions, and to handle interpersonal relationships judiciously and empathetically.

**17. Ethical Dilemma:** A situation in which a difficult choice has to be made between two or more alternatives, especially equally undesirable ones, involving a conflict of moral principles.

By exploring these concepts through the lens of project management, the book aims to offer readers a comprehensive framework for integrating spiritual wisdom with practical strategies, enhancing leadership effectiveness and personal growth.